English for academic study:
Reading

Course Book

John Slaght and Paddy Harben

Centre for Applied Language Studies

University of
Reading

Credits

Published by
Garnet Publishing Ltd.
8 Southern Court
South Street
Reading RG1 4QS, UK

First published 2004
Second edition published 2006
Reprinted 2008
ISBN-13: 978 1 85964 836 0

British Cataloguing-in-Publication Data
A catalogue record for this book is available from
the British Library.

Production

Project manager:	Richard Peacock
Project consultant:	Rod Webb
Editorial team:	Lucy Thompson, Angela Langridge, Francesca Pinagli
Design:	Mike Hinks
Illustration:	Mike Hinks, Doug Nash
Photography:	Corbis: Robert Essel NYC, Jeremy Horner, Caroline Penn, Michael Prince, Franco Vogt, Roger Wilmshurst; Mike Hinks; The United Nations.

Every effort has been made to trace the copyright holders
and we apologize in advance for any unintentional
omission. We will be happy to insert the appropriate
acknowledgements in any subsequent editions.

Printed and bound
by Ruscombe Litho and Digital Printing Ltd.

The authors and publishers wish to acknowledge the
following use of material:

'Economics focus: On the move' © The Economist
Newspaper Limited, London (May 12th, 2001).

'Does Class Size Matter?' reprinted with permission.
Copyright © 2001 by *Scientific American*, Inc.
All rights reserved.

Atkinson, R.L. *et al.*, *Hilgard's Introduction to Psychology*,
13th edition (1999). © 1996. Reprinted with permission
of Wadsworth, a division of Thomson Learning:
www.thomsonrights.com. Fax 800 730-2215

Middleton, N., 'Acid rain in Norway' in *Geography
Review*, Vol. 11, No. 4. (1998) Reprinted with permission
© Philip Allan Updates.

Everett, M., 'Impact – Skylarks in decline' in *Biological
Sciences Review*, Vol. 10, No. 2. (1997) Reprinted with
permission © Philip Allan Updates.

'Statistics Without Tears: A Primer for Non-Mathematicians'
by Derek Rowntree (Penguin Books, 1982). Copyright ©
Derek Rowntree, 1982. Pages 14–21 reproduced by
permission of Penguin Books Ltd.

'Common Questions about Climate Change'
(pages 4–12), reprinted with permission © United
Nations Environment Programme and World
Meteorological Organization.

'The Global Village: Challenges for a Shrinking
Planet', reprinted with permission from *The Global
Village: Challenges for a Shrinking Planet* (*Understanding
Global Issues 98/7*).

'The New Linguistic Order' in *Foreign Policy*, Winter
1998–99 (pages 26–39), Joshua A. Fishman

Contents

Acknowledgements

The Reading course has been developed to dovetail with the Writing course produced by CALS colleague, Anne Pallant. Anne has played a major role in reviewing material at every stage of development and helping refine the rationale behind the reading into writing approach.

Further significant cooperation in reviewing and editing the materials has come from present and former colleagues at CALS, particularly Ros Richards, Joan McCormack, Colin Campbell, Paul Stocks, Heather Bagley and Sarah Brewer.

In the production of the pilot editions, Paul Thompson contributed considerable IT support and Jill Riley showed great patience and good humour in her painstaking editing and typing.

Pre-sessional teachers in 2000–2005 gave invaluable feedback during trialling of the texts, tasks and teacher's notes.

Many thanks to all the above and also to the many hundreds of students who have already worked with pilot editions of these materials.

A big apology to anyone I have omitted from this list.

John Slaght, Author, February 2006,
Centre for Applied Languages Studies,
University of Reading, UK

Reference to Source Book texts

Introduction

In this course you will be working on four main aspects of academic reading:
- Reading for a specific academic purpose
- Working on specific strategies that are associated with effective and successful reading
- Detailed comprehension of sentences and paragraphs
- Text analysis

Let's look at each of these in detail, as they will be referred to again during the course.

1. Reading for a specific academic purpose

Here you will be concentrating on getting information from the text which will help you complete an academic task. There are many academic tasks that involve reading.
For example, you may need to:

- complete an assignment on a specific question, for which it is necessary to combine information from various sources (e.g. to submit an essay or give a spoken presentation);

- get an introductory overview of a new topic in order to assist with listening to a series of lectures on that topic;

- add new knowledge about a topic to what you already know. This could be, for example, note-taking for future exam revision or simply reading a text and thinking about what you have read in order to understand the topic better.

2. Working on specific strategies that are associated with effective and successful reading

The main strategies we will be looking at are:

- **Skimming** Looking at a text *very* quickly in order to do one or more of the following:
  - Identify what the text is about (the topic)
  - Identify the main idea of the text
  - Decide how useful the text is for your purposes
  - Decide how you will make use of the text

  Skimming a text might involve looking at some or all of the following features of the text:

  - Title
  - Section headings
  - Abstract or summary provided by the writer
  - First and last paragraphs
  - First and last sentences of intervening paragraphs
  - Concentrating on the topic sentences in each paragraph. These are sometimes referred to as 'paragraph leaders'.

  Another form of skimming is when you are previewing a book in order to decide how useful it is for your purposes. In this situation, you might also look at one or more of the following:

  - Information about the author and/or publication details
  - Contents page
  - Foreword and/or Introduction
  - Index

- **Predicting** Using what you already know about the topic, what you want to learn about the topic from the text, and what you have learnt from your previewing in order to guess what kind of information the text will contain and how useful it will be. You will often be surprised how much you already know about a text before you even begin reading. Brainstorming your 'prior' knowledge will help you to understand the text – at least at the surface level.

- **Scanning** Finding *words* (or other symbols, such as figures) which have particular importance for you, the reader. When you are scanning, you already know the form of the words or symbols you are looking for. This is a bit like using word-processing, when you ask the program to search the document on screen for a particular word or phrase. When you scan, you normally focus on small parts of the text only.

- **Search reading** Quickly finding *ideas* which are particularly important for you. This is different from scanning, because you don't know the exact words you are looking for in advance, so you cannot make a direct match. When you search read, you normally ignore a lot of the text.

- **Identifying the main ideas** Understanding the writer's main points. It may be possible to do this quite quickly after skimming the text. However, with more difficult texts it may only be possible to identify the main ideas after more detailed reading.

- **Careful reading** Reading slowly and carefully so that you understand every word in the text (or the part of the text that you are most interested in). You might do this in order to understand the details of the text and also to infer meaning that has not been directly stated (see below).

- **Inferring** Obtaining meaning from the text that the writer has not explicitly stated. You may have to infer different types of meaning. For example:

  - Sometimes the writer expects you to fill gaps in the text in order for it to make sense. Example: *The invention of the steam engine had a major effect on society.* The reader must infer that it is not just the *invention* that affected society, but *the way it was used*.

  - Sometimes you may wish to infer *why* the writer wrote the text (i.e. the writer's purpose). Connected to this, you may wish to infer the writer's *attitude* to what he or she is writing about.

- **Dealing with unfamiliar words** When you find a word you don't understand in a text, you need to decide first whether it is really necessary to understand the word. Perhaps you can understand enough of the text without understanding the word, in which case you can ignore it. Alternatively, the context in which the word is located may allow you to guess the meaning of the word well enough to continue reading. If neither of these applies, you may have to look up the word in a dictionary. If you find you are using a dictionary so much that you are prevented from reading the text at a reasonable speed, the text may be too specialised for you, and you should consider finding another one which deals with the same topic in a more generalised way.

  An approach to dealing with new vocabulary is to decide whether:

  - you need to know the word **now** to help you understand the text **and** use it **later** under different circumstances. In this case, you will need some way of recording the word, e.g. in a vocabulary notebook. In this case, you will have to decide whether to rely on working out the meaning of the word from context, or whether you need to check the meaning in a dictionary;

  - you **only** need to know the word **now** to help you understand the text. This is often the case with technical words or low-frequency words. These are words which are not often used in English, even by native speakers of the language, unless for specialist reasons. Of course, if you are reading a text in your academic area, you may need to know certain specialist vocabulary and not only record it, but use this vocabulary so that it becomes part of your **active** vocabulary, i.e. words that you use regularly in order to communicate effectively;

  - you **don't** need to know this word either now or in the future. If you feel the word does not prevent you from understanding the rest of the text, then you probably do not need to worry about this word. If the word occurs several times in the text, however, you may feel it is necessary to work out its meaning or look it up and record it.

3. Detailed comprehension of sentences and paragraphs

A lot of your work will involve dealing with complete texts and getting information from them in various ways. However, in order to do this it may at times be necessary to have a very precise understanding of specific sentences and paragraphs. This may be difficult in terms of either grammar or ideas, of organisation or because of a combination of these.

4. Text analysis

It is often helpful to understand the way a text is organised in order to make the best use of it. The organisation of a text can be considered at the global level; for example, the way that the text is organised into sections and paragraphs according to the purpose of the text and the type of text. In a report of an experiment, for example, it is very common to see the following pattern of organisation:

- Title
- Abstract
- Introduction/background
- Method
- Results
- Conclusions
- References/bibliography

Another aspect of organisation that can be useful to examine is how information is organised logically at the local level within complex sentences or paragraphs. For example, the following sentence taken from *Hilgard's Introduction to Psychology*, 12th edition by Atkinson. © 1996.

> The question of whether heredity ("nature") or environment ("nurture") is more important in determining the course of human development has been debated through the centuries.

If this sentence seems difficult to understand, its organisation can be identified as **x has been y**, as in

- **x** [The question of whether heredity ("nature") or environment ("nurture") is more important in determining the course of human development]

- has been
  y [debated through the centuries.]

As you can see, there are many different aspects of academic reading that we will be considering during the course. Whilst it is important to be aware of all these different things, it is also important to:

- develop a flexible reading style. Becoming a better academic reader is not just about mastering different aspects of reading. It is also important to decide which is the best way to read a text depending on the particular academic purpose that you have for reading it. This will be stressed a great deal during the course;

- remember that the more you read, the better you will read. Regular independent reading outside the classroom is essential for any student wishing to develop reading abilities such as fluency, greater reading speed, vocabulary acquisition and the strategies associated with successful reading. You can improve your academic reading level by making decisions about:

  - *why* you are reading;
  - *what* you are reading;
  - *how* you are reading;
  - *how well* you are reading.

Task introduction

Economics focus: On the move

In the accompanying *Reading and Writing Source Book* (pages 5–6), you will find a sample reading text through which you will practise some of the skills and strategies outlined in the Introduction on pages 7–9 of this book.

Task 1: Deciding if a text is useful

Imagine you need some information because you are going to attend an Economic History lecture about the link between migration and economic forces. This is a new subject for you, and you want to have some background information before attending your first lecture.

You have found a number of articles on the subject, but you don't have time to read them all, so you have to decide which ones to read. The article *Economics focus: On the move* is an introduction to one of the articles you have selected for background reading. You have to decide whether the whole article would be useful. We will go through the stages that will help you make that decision.

1.1 Look only at the parts of the article in the *Reading Source Book* which have been printed in *italics*. Looking at these parts of the article will provide you with important information about the text. For example, you may work out who the intended reader is.

Who is the intended reader?

a) a business analyst

b) an educated general reader

c) an Economics student

d) a historian

Write down one reason for your choice:

_____

_____

_____

_____

_____

1.2 Without reading the whole text, but only the parts in italics, what could you guess about its content and the way it will be organised? Write down as many ideas as you can. The important thing is to start thinking about the text before you read it and to predict what it may contain.

_____

_____

_____

_____

_____

_____

1.3 Read through the text and highlight any sections of the text which are similar to the ideas that you predicted. Don't worry too much about vocabulary at the moment, as you are just reading to get an overall (global) understanding of the text. Some vocabulary will be looked at in Task 2.

As you work through the following tasks, you can check the accuracy of your predictions.

Task 2: Word-building from a text

You will have noticed the word *immigration* in the subtitle. Scan through the text to find all the examples of this word being used. Note the line number and highlight the word and any words that seem to go with it. Also look for similar words, e.g. *migration* (line 5). The word *migration* is a noun, and in line 18 the word is connected to the verb *to restrict*. Use three of the different forms of the word *immigration* you find to complete the table below

2.1

Word used	Line number	Word class	Connected language
migration	line 18	noun	to restrict migration

2.2 You have probably realised that nearly all the words you have found to complete the table are nouns. What verbs or adjectives could you form from the words you have used to complete the table? For example, *to migrate*; *people first migrated to America in the 17th century.*

Make up your own sentences to show how verbs or adjectives can be formed from the words in the table.

Task 3: Identifying the organisation of a text

3.1 How is the text *Economics focus: On the move* divided up?

3.2 Clearly the text is divided into two parts. Where does this division into two parts occur? Discuss with a partner and then check with your teacher.

Look more closely at the first part of the text. Look specifically at the first paragraph. What is the main idea in this paragraph? Again discuss the answer with a partner before checking with your teacher.

The main idea is _____

_____

_____

_____

Now look at paragraphs 2–5. What is the main purpose of these paragraphs? As above, discuss the answer with your partner and then check with the teacher.

The purpose of paragraphs 2–5 is _____

_____

_____

_____

3.3 Look more closely at the second part of the text. What appears to be the main purpose of the second half of the text?

Highlight some words, phrases or even sentences in the text to support what you think is the main purpose of the second part of the text.

The main purpose of the second half of the text is _____

_____

_____

_____

Check with a partner and then discuss with your teacher.

Task 4: Writing a summary of part of the text

4.1 How well have you understood the first part of the text as far as line 98? Reread this part of the text in order to understand the main ideas more clearly.

When you have finished reading, try to complete the summary on page 13.

Use one, two or three words in the gaps. The first gap has been completed as an example.

There is a clear link between the history of migration to America and ❶ economic factors. At first, migration to America was very expensive and migrants were usually ❷ _____ or indentured labourers. However, as travel became easier, many more people ❸ _____ . This continued throughout ❹ _____ and early 20ᵗʰ century, but then war and ❺ _____ slowed down and even reversed migratory trends. After the Second World War, ❻ _____ increased again.

4.2 Now see how well you have understood the second part of the text. Reread this part of the text in order to understand the main ideas more clearly.

Paragraph matching: label the paragraphs, beginning at line 100, A–G.

Three of the paragraphs are summarised below, but are not in the order of the text. Match these summaries to three of the paragraphs A–G.

- Countries all over the world have experienced economic growth, and this factor is likely to encourage another wave of migration.

- Countries with the greatest wealth are now in a position to be selective in the type of immigrant they want. This is good for these countries, but causes greater problems for the poorest, least-skilled migrants.

- Both the immigrants involved and the countries where they migrate to can benefit from the migration of labour. However, at first, the workforce in these countries tends to suffer.

Task 5: Dealing with unknown vocabulary

This activity will help you practise the technique for dealing with unknown vocabulary described on page 8.

5.1 The following words and phrases appear in the text *Economics focus: On the move*:

makes plain (line 25); harsh (line 36); indentured (line 43); slavery (line 49); falling (line 65); comparatively (line 75–76); net (line 79); feasible (line 91); expansionary (line 124)

5.2 Which of these words do you already know?

5.3 Find the words in the text and decide whether **(A)** you need to know the word now and add it to your active vocabulary; **(B)** you only need to know this word now because it is preventing you from understanding the general meaning of the text; or **(C)** you don't need to know this word or add it to your active vocabulary.

5.4 Complete the table by placing a tick (✓) in either Column A, B or C.

Vocabulary	Column A	Column B	Column C	Word class*
makes plain				
harsh				
indentured				
slavery				
falling				
comparatively				
net				
feasible				
expansionary				

*Word class: All words belong to a particular word class. Word class is sometimes referred to as *part of speech*. Look at the following phrase from the text.

> The <u>world</u> (n) <u>has experienced</u> (vb) a new (adj) <u>era</u> of <u>globalisation</u> (—), <u>which</u> (—) <u>is</u> (—) <u>much</u> (—) <u>quicker</u> (—).

Can you add the word class of the underlined words? The first three have been done for you.

5.5 Now complete the final column of the table by filling in the word class. Try to do this by finding the words in the text and working out the word class from its position in relation to other words and its function in the text.

> Identifying word class can help you work out the meaning of a particular word.Use the following abbreviations:
> n = noun; pron = pronoun; adj = adjective; adv = adverb

Task 6: Evaluating the level of content

> When deciding how useful a text is for your academic reading purpose, it is often useful to think about the writer's attitude to the topic and his or her purpose for writing it.

What do you think was the writer's attitude and purpose when writing *Economics focus: On the move*? Read through the text one more time and decide which of the following you most agree with. Write down any ideas you have about the writer's attitude and purpose so that you can defend your opinion in a class discussion.

a) To inform the reader about the topic

b) To persuade the reader to accept his or her opinion

c) To challenge ideas about the topic

d) To give a balanced opinion about the topic

e) To do all of these things

f) To do some of these things

My views on the writer's attitude and purpose: _____

_____

_____

_____

_____

_____

_____

_____

_____

_____

_____

_____

_____

_____

Task 7: Reading for a purpose

With the whole class, or with a partner, discuss the following:

Looking back at the tasks you have done, is the text *Economics focus: On the move* suitable for your reading purpose? (Your reading purpose was to get some background information before attending a lecture on migration and economic forces.)

Why is it suitable? or Why is it not suitable?

Summarise your answer in one sentence below:

_____

_____

_____

_____

_____

Task 8: Reviewing reading styles

You are now going to reflect on the activities you have carried out in this unit.

8.1 In small groups or pairs, discuss some or all of the following questions:

a) Why is it useful to predict the contents of a text before reading it?

b) What are reading strategies? How can they help the reader?

c) What is global understanding of a text? Why is it useful to get a global understanding of a text?

d) Why is reading very slowly through a text word by word often an unsuccessful reading strategy?

e) Why is it often important to read only parts of a text?

f) Why is it useful to consider who the intended reader is before starting to read a text?

8.2 With the whole class, or with the members of your group, discuss the suggested answers that your teacher will give you. Make a note of important ideas below.

1 Academic achievement

The topic of this unit concerns factors which may lead to improved academic performance among students. It is based on three major research projects carried out in the United States.

This unit will give you practice in:

- using your prior knowledge to help you understand what you are reading;
- reading for a specific purpose;
- making decisions about the relevance of a text in terms of reading purpose;
- reading selectively in order to use appropriate information from the text.

Pre-reading task: Predicting text content

- Think about what factors in a school, college or university can have an influence on the academic achievements of the students.
- Look at the following list of possible influences and rate the ideas on a scale of 1–5, where (1) means 'very little influence' and (5) means 'very strong influence'.
- Add some ideas of your own and rate them as well.

Influence on academic performance	Rating
Resources available (e.g. computers, laboratories, textbooks)	① ② ③ ④ ⑤
Teacher level (qualifications, experience, etc.)	① ② ③ ④ ⑤
Student motivation	① ② ③ ④ ⑤
	① ② ③ ④ ⑤
	① ② ③ ④ ⑤
	① ② ③ ④ ⑤

- Compare your list and the ratings with a partner.
- Keep a note of your ratings for a later activity.

Text 1–1 | The influence of class size on academic achievement (Source Book pp. 7–9)

Reading task 1: Reading for a purpose

Your reason for reading this text is to get some background information to help you write the following essay:

What are the aims of academic study and how can they be achieved?

1.1 Look carefully at the title of the text in the *Reading and Writing Source Book*. Do you now think that the text will be useful for writing an assignment about academic achievement?

1.2 Read the introduction to the article (lines 1–66). As you read, try to make up your mind about how useful this text might be for your purpose.

1.3 When you have finished reading, complete the following sentence:

The text may/will/will not be useful because _____

_____

_____

Reading task 2: Reading selectively

You are now going to read the next two sections of the article (lines 67–192).

2.1 First, you are going to study lines 67–117. Look at the subheading. Do you think that smaller class sizes help to improve academic performance?

YES/NO/NOT SURE (Underline your view at this stage.)

Write down one reason for your answer in a short sentence.

_____

_____

_____

2.2 Below are some notes on this text made by a student. Read lines 67–117 and decide which of the points listed are mentioned in the text.

a) Easier to concentrate

b) Students prefer smaller classes

c) More cooperative learning occurs

d) More help for students with problems

e) Students develop good methods of learning

f) More opportunities to use resources if fewer students in class

g) Students get much better academic results

2.3 Look at the first sentence of the first paragraph (lines 69–72).

What does *anecdotal* mean? You may need to check this word in a dictionary, but first try to guess the meaning of this word by looking carefully at the whole sentence.

If the ideas in this paragraph are *anecdotal*, how seriously should you believe them for your assignment?

2.4 Look at the first sentence of the second paragraph (lines 97–100).

How useful do you think this paragraph might be in relation to your writing assignment?

Underline specific information which you might use from this paragraph to help in the completion of the assignment.

With a partner, compare and justify your choice of information for all four questions.

Reading task 3: Identifying the writer's purpose

You are now going to read the next section of the text (lines 118–192).

3.1 It is often very important to recognise why the writer has written a text, or a section of a text (i.e. what the function of the text is).

As you read, try to decide what the main function of this section of text is from the choices given below.

For each choice, rate the function from 0–5 depending on how sure you are (5 = very sure).

To persuade the readers to accept a certain point of view	① ② ③ ④ ⑤
To explain the importance of using research data instead of *anecdotal* explanations	① ② ③ ④ ⑤
To evaluate the importance of the research carried out into the effect of classroom size on academic achievement	① ② ③ ④ ⑤
To describe the research method used in various parts of the U.S. into the effect of classroom size on academic achievement	① ② ③ ④ ⑤

3.2 What is the function (or functions) of Figure 1: *Milestone studies in class size*?

a) To summarise the content of the text

b) To outline the content of certain relevant research

c) To explain the importance of the STAR project

d) To compare the data from research about class size

Reading task 4: Understanding referencing in text and note-taking

In this task, you are going to look at referencing in a text. Referencing is a way of linking words and ideas together, thus making the text more cohesive and, therefore, easier to understand.

4.1 Look at line 119. What information or idea in the text do the words *these findings* refer to?

a) The U.S. Department of Education

b) The National Assessment of Educational Progress

c) Project STAR

4.2 What other words or phrases (lines 119–148) refer to the same data?

a) _____ (line number _____)

b) _____ (line number _____)

4.3 What reasons do the writers give for ignoring these data? Complete the list below, using a similar note form.

a) Decreased dropout rates

b) _____

c) _____

d) _____

e) More experienced teachers

4.4 What factors, according to the writers, made Project STAR better than other *poorly designed* studies? Complete the list below, using a similar note form.

a) _____

b) The research was carried out over 3 years

c) _____

d) _____

e) No new curricular methods

Text 1–2   A case study: Shining star (Source Book p. 10)

Reading task 1: Reading a text for closer understanding

1.1 What general point is made in the first paragraph of this section (lines 1–11)?

Find a short phrase which best summarises this conclusion.

_____

_____

1.2 Which of the following benefits of smaller classes do Finn and Achilles identify in their review of the project? Answer either *TRUE* or *FALSE*. Indicate the line number where you found your answer.

a) Better academic performance in small-sized classes. _____

b) Students benefit at an early stage in small classes. _____

c) Students later continue to perform well in normal-sized classes. _____

d) Average students make the most progress. _____

e) Minority groups gained the most significant benefit. _____

f) On average, ethnic minority students improved by one-fifth of standard deviation. _____

1.3 Which of the findings of Finn and Achilles does Hanushek comment on?

Put a tick (✓) when Hanushek agrees and a cross (✗) when he disagrees and note the line number where his view is stated in the text. Put N/A if Hanushek doesn't mention these findings.

a) _____ (line number _____)

b) _____ (line number _____)

c) _____ (line number _____)

d) _____ (line number _____)

e) _____ (line number _____)

f) _____ (line number _____)

1.4 To what extent do you feel that the analyses of Project STAR will help you with your writing assignment (i.e. **What are the aims of academic study and how can they be achieved?**)?

Rate your opinion 0–5 (0 = not at all).

Discuss your rating with a partner.

Text 1-3 | The Asian paradox: Huge classes, high scores (Source Book p. 11)

Reading task 1: Reading a text for closer understanding

1.1 As a Pre-reading exercise, discuss either in pairs or in groups what you know about academic performance in developed Asian countries, and how academic success is achieved.

1.2 You are now going to read lines 1–65. As you read, remember to highlight ideas which might be useful for your writing assignment.

1.3 What is the 'Asian paradox'?

What <u>one</u> word in the text (lines 17–35) is used as <u>one</u> explanation for this contradictory statement?

1.4 Find other short phrases in the rest of this paragraph (lines 35–48) which might provide further reasons for the apparent academic success of Japanese students. List these below.

a) _____

b) _____

c) _____

d) _____

e) _____

1.5 Having read the text, have you found any information which might be useful for your writing assignment?

Reading task 2: Thinking critically about the text

Return to the Pre-reading task on page 17.

2.1 Look at the list of possible influences on academic performance which you rated.

2.2 Are there any new influences you would like to add to the table, and any which you wish to delete?

2.3 If you added any influences to your table, what rating would you give them?

Influence on academic performance	Rating
	① ② ③ ④ ⑤
	① ② ③ ④ ⑤
	① ② ③ ④ ⑤
	① ② ③ ④ ⑤
	① ② ③ ④ ⑤
	① ② ③ ④ ⑤

Reading task 3: Making use of the text

You now have some information that may help with the writing assignment which you will be given in order to complete Unit 1 of *English for academic study: Writing*, if you are studying that course.

What you must decide is if, and how, you can use the information in this text.

2 Early human development

The topic of this unit is how humans develop at an early age, focusing on the relationship between *nature* and *nurture*.

This unit will give you practice in:

- making use of the knowledge you already have about a topic before you read more about it;
- recognising key words and finding out the meaning of difficult/unfamiliar words that are important for helping you achieve your purpose for reading;
- quickly understanding the main points of the text that you are reading;
- reading parts of a text more carefully in order to fully make use of it according to your purpose;
- summarising useful information that you have found in a text.

Pre-reading task 1: Accessing background knowledge

1.1 The following is the first sentence of a text about nature and nurture:

The question of whether heredity ("nature") or environment ("nurture") is more important in determining the course of human development has been debated through the centuries.
Atkinson, R. L. *et al.*, *Hilgard's Introduction to Psychology*, 13ᵗʰ edition (1999). © 1996.

How much do you already know about this topic?

a) Nothing

b) A little

c) Quite a lot

d) A lot

1.2 Which do you think is more important in determining the course of human development? Choose one of the following answers:

a) Nature is the most important.

b) Nurture is the most important.

c) Nature and nurture are equally important.

d) I'm not sure.

Pre-reading task 2: Vocabulary development

2.1 The following words (**a–t**) all occur in Text 2–1. Match these words with the definitions (**1–20**). Write the appropriate numbers in the horizontal box at the bottom of the page. Use a dictionary when necessary.

a	nature	**1**	a baby before it is born
b	nurture	**2**	the effect of one thing on another
c	senses	**3**	an infectious illness
d	malleable	**4**	egg
e	heredity	**5**	to get faster
f	personality traits	**6**	inborn, already present at the time of birth
g	environment	**7**	inheriting characteristics from previous generations
h	genetic	**8**	natural processes
i	innate	**9**	permanent characteristics of somebody's behaviour
j	biological	**10**	processes caused by surroundings
k	ovum	**11**	related to brain processes
l	fetus	**12**	related to language, especially when it is spoken
m	German measles	**13**	related to the mother
n	maternal	**14**	relating to the information that is coded in the cells of the body
o	interaction	**15**	to repeat a skill to improve it
p	to practise	**16**	sight, taste, touch, etc.
q	to accelerate	**17**	surroundings
r	neurological	**18**	to bring up or educate (children)
s	to rear	**19**	to do with the physical processes of living things
t	verbal	**20**	very flexible and changeable

a	b	c	d	e	f	g	h	i	j	k	l	m	n	o	p	q	r	s	t

2.2 Find the words from the list above and underline them in Text 2–1 (pages 12–13).

2.3 The following words are defined in the text. Find them in the text and write an appropriate definition for each.

maturation	
motor behaviours	

Reading task 1: Reading for general understanding

Read through Text 2–1 in order to get a general idea about the contents. As you read, compare the content of the text with the ideas you had in the first two pre-reading tasks. The vocabulary work you did in the second two pre-reading tasks should help your understanding of the text.

Reading task 2: Developing further understanding

Read the names and terms in the box below:

John Locke	modern psychologists	Darwin	Skinner & Watson

2.1 Read paragraphs A–C of the text. Which of the people named above are connected with the following ideas? Some ideas may relate to more than one of them.

a) A scientific explanation that supported the view that nature was more important than nurture in human development.

b) Human development is determined entirely by experience.

c) Human development can be easily influenced or changed.

d) Both hereditary and environmental factors are important in human development.

2.2 Read the remaining paragraphs of the text (paragraphs D–H). Which paragraph talks about the following?

a) The unchanging stages in the learning of motor skills.

b) Nature's role in shaping certain basic physical features.

c) The development of language skills.

d) The effect of environmental factors such as illness or the habits of the mother on natural human development.

e) The effects of training on motor skills.

Reading task 3: Understanding the main argument

Look at the following sentences and decide which one summarises the main argument of the text most accurately.

a) Most experts today agree that babies mainly develop as a result of the environment in which they live, and that the type of adult they become is determined by the early training they are given.

b) According to current opinion, a combination of natural development before and after birth, and the experiences which infants have, influence their processes of maturation.

c) Today, scientists believe that humans evolve into their final adult form as the result of biological processes which alone determine the development of motor skills and the ability to speak.

d) There have been many debates about the main influences on early human development throughout history, and even now, many scientists are unable to agree about this issue.

Reading task 4: Note-taking from the text

Imagine that you are writing an essay about early human development. You have decided to include a table which summarises the ways in which it may be influenced by nature and nurture. Complete the table below, referring back to the text as necessary.

Table 1: The influences of nature and nurture on early human development

Influences of nature on early human development	Influences of nurture on early human development
Genetic structure of fertilised ovum determines sex of fetus, colour of hair, general body size, etc.	Abnormal uterine environment can affect maturation process, e.g. if mother contracts German measles.

Hilgard's Introduction to Psychology, 12ᵗʰ edition by Atkinson. © 1996. pp 70–71.

Reading task 5: Developing understanding of the text

Read the whole text again and choose the time periods from the box that correspond to the ideas below. Some ideas may relate to more than one time period.

| 17th century | 19th century | 1930s | second half of 20th century |

a)   Children's development can be completely shaped by training.

b)   If children are given practical encouragement, they will learn to walk more quickly.

c)   Human development only occurs after birth.

d)   The hereditary view supports the biological theory.

e)   Encouragement from people can speed up children's development of speech.

f)   Children have inherited characteristics which develop naturally after birth, but are not influenced by the environment.

g)   Environmental factors can affect human development before birth.

Reading task 6: Working with words from the text

6.1   Sort the words in the box below into groups of related meanings. You may decide you need a number of different groups, and some words may come into more than one group

to accelerate	biological	environment	fetus	genetic
German measles	heredity	innate	interaction	malleable
maternal	nature	neurological	nurture	ovum
personality traits	to practise	to rear	senses	verbal

6.2   Which words do not seem to fit into any of your word groups?

_____

_____

_____

_____

_____

_____

_____

_____

_____

6.3   Explain your word groups to a partner.

This section concerns the capacities of newborn babies, still within the overall topic of early human development. There is a focus on search reading and summarising useful information found in a text.

Pre-reading task

In your opinion, how well prepared are newborn babies to learn from their environment? Which of the following do you think is most likely?

- They are poorly prepared and are totally confused by what is going on around them.
- They are well prepared and are ready to learn quickly.

Discuss your answer with your group.

Reading task 1: Inferring meaning from the text

1.1   Read paragraph A of Text 2–2: *Capacities of the newborn*. What are the *sensory systems* mentioned by the writer?

1.2   What is the writer's answer to the question in the Pre-reading task?

Reading task 2: Summarising information from the text

2.1   Don't continue reading at this point, but think about the following question:

How do you think psychologists know that newborn babies are "well prepared to learn about their new environment"?

What kind of experiments do you think psychologists might have done to find out?

2.2   Now read paragraph B of Text 2–2. Your purpose is to find out about the ways that psychologists have investigated how well prepared newborn babies are to learn from their new environment. Imagine that you have to explain and exemplify this to a friend. Highlight the key words that give you the information you need.

2.3   Compare your key words with those of the rest of the class, and discuss why you have chosen them.

2.4   Write a one-sentence summary using your key words, without referring back to the text.

2.5   Compare your summary with the rest of the class.

Reading task 3: Summarising information from the text

3.1 The next section of Text 2–2 is about vision. What features of the visual environment do you think most catch the attention of newborn babies?

3.2 Find the answer to this question in paragraphs C–E and highlight the key words that give you this information.

3.3 Write a one-sentence summary of the answer to the above question using your key words, without referring back to the text. Compare your answer with your partner.

_____

_____

Text 2–3 | Hearing, taste and smell (Source Book p. 15)

This section expands on the capacities of newborn babies. There is a focus on search reading and summarising text-based discussion.

Pre-reading task

What can newborn babies do in terms of hearing, taste and smell? Put a tick (✓) against the following things that you think newborn babies (aged one month or less) can do:

a) Hear loud noises ☐

b) Turn their heads towards where a sound is coming from ☐

c) Correctly identify where a sound is coming from in the dark ☐

d) See the difference between a picture of a cat and a picture of a dog ☐

e) Hear the difference between two sounds that are almost the same ☐

f) Hear the difference between speech and non-human sounds ☐

g) Hear the difference between some sounds better than adults can ☐

h) Tell the difference between hot and cold food ☐

i) Taste the difference between sweet, sour and bitter-tasting things ☐

j) Smell the difference between their mother's milk and milk from a bottle ☐

k) Tell the difference between the smell of a banana and the smell of a peach ☐

l) Tell the difference between a nice smell and an unpleasant smell ☐

Reading task 1: Reading for a purpose and creating a summary

1.1 Now read Text 2–3: *Hearing, taste and smell*, and find out which of the above activities newborn babies can do, according to the writer.

1.2 Do any of these things that babies can do surprise or interest you? Discuss in groups. If your answer is NO, try to explain why you are not surprised or interested. Where necessary, refer to the text in order to support your point of view.

1.3 Basically, the text suggests that babies have four innate abilities related to hearing, taste and smell. Write a short paragraph summarising these innate qualities that babies seem to be born with. For example, according to paragraph A, newborn babies react to noise.

Write your summary below.

3a The environment today

In this unit you will read two texts. The first text is called *Acid rain in Norway* and the second is called *Skylarks in decline*.

This unit will give you practice in:

- reading quickly for global comprehension of the main ideas in a text;
- making use of your prior knowledge to help your global comprehension;
- identifying key words to enhance quick global comprehension;
- carrying out a reading skill which is often useful for academic reading tests;
- thinking about what strategies to use for a specific reading purpose.

Text 3a–1 Acid rain in Norway (Source Book pp. 16–17)

Pre-reading task: Raising text awareness

1.1 What is a global summary? Write a one-sentence definition below.

_____

_____

Often it is useful to be able to summarise a text quickly and efficiently without carefully reading all or nearly all of the words in the text. You are going to practise this in the following text.

When you want to globally summarise a text, you need to focus immediately on the topic. Thus, the title should help. You may find as a result of reading the title that you will automatically draw on your prior knowledge to bring what you know about the topic to mind. In this case, your prior knowledge will be anything you already know about *acid rain*.

1.2 Turn to Text 3a–1 on pages 16–17 in the *Reading and Writing Source Book*. What is the title? Using the lines below, you have one minute to write down anything you know about *acid rain*.

_____

_____

_____

_____

You may also want to ask yourself questions about the title, e.g. *Is acid rain only important in Norway?*

1.3 What other questions might you ask yourself about the title?
Discuss your ideas with another student.

Using overt information

Text 3a–1 contains quite a lot of *overt* or *displayed* information, e.g. apart from the title, there are also three figures, a table and two section subheadings. Figure 1, for example, tells you that the use of lime to reduce acidification damage in Norway seems to have increased significantly between 1983 and 1995 (particularly after 1993). Therefore, certain key words may be useful here and in the other sources of *overt* information provided with this text. Terms such as *lime* and *acidification damage* are obviously important, and are phrases which you might focus on in order to gain a quick global understanding of the text.

Reading task 1: Taking information from displayed information

1.1 Look through Text 3a–1. What new information (or words) do you learn from Figures 2 and 3, Table 1 and the two section subheadings? For example, what trends do the figures suggest?

Information source	New information or words
Section subheading A	
Section subheading B	
Figure 1	*Very sharp rise in amount of lime used to reduce acidification damage – especially since 1993.*
Figure 2	
Figure 3	
Table 1	

1.2 Before looking at the rest of *Acid rain in Norway*, discuss in small groups ways of quickly finding information that will help you form a global summary of a text. Complete the following summary box, using the information above and any other ideas that your group suggested.

Ways of quickly accessing information about a text include:

❶ looking at the title

❷ _____

❸ _____

❹ _____

❺ _____

❻ _____

Reading task 2: Writing a global summary

2.1 Your teacher will now set you a time limit to learn as much as you can about the text *Acid rain in Norway* on pages 16–17.

2.2 Your teacher will now tell you how long you have to write a single-paragraph summary of the text. When writing, concentrate on the main points. Write as accurately as you can, but your main aim is to communicate as clearly as you can what you've understood as the main point(s) of the text within the time limit.

_____

_____

_____

_____

_____

_____

_____

_____

_____

_____

_____

2.3 Compare your summary with the model supplied by the teacher.

2.4 Consider the following questions:

- Do you agree with the teacher's summary?
- What strategy or strategies did you use to carry out the task?
- Was/Were the strategy or strategies successful?

2.5 How successful was your summary? Tick below:

a) 100% ☐ **b)** 75% ☐ **c)** 50% ☐ **d)** 25% ☐

2.6 If you had any problems with the text, what were they? Tick below:

a) Difficulty with the topic ☐

b) Difficulty with the vocabulary and/or the language ☐

c) The way the text was organised ☐

d) Difficulty with the content of the text (e.g. ideas, hypothesis, concepts, etc.) ☐

e) The length of the text ☐

f) Other reasons (not listed above)

Text 3a–2 | Skylarks in decline (Source Book pp. 18–20)

You now have a second text to globally summarise: *Skylarks in decline*.

Reading task 1: More global summary practice

1.1 Turn to the *Reading and Writing Source Book*. Your teacher will give you a time limit to read this text and write a one-paragraph summary, using your own words. You will not have time to read the whole text.

1.2 Compare your summary with the model supplied by the teacher. It is important to appreciate that this is not necessarily the only way to globally summarise this text. Remember that this is a reading activity, and your main focus of comparison should be the content of your summary, not the accuracy of your language.

1.3 Finally, discuss the following questions:

● In what ways was this text similar or different to *Acid rain in Norway*?

● What strategy or strategies did you employ for completing this task?

● Were you more or less successful in completing this second text?

SUMMARISING A TEXT

When summarising a text, or part of a text, it's important to understand that not all of the strategies suggested in this unit for quickly finding out the main points will be successful every time. For example, looking at the first sentence of each paragraph of *Skylarks in decline* does not necessarily help you to find the main point of each paragraph. However, looking at the first sentence of each paragraph does help you find the main points in the *Acid rain in Norway* text. If you experiment with the reading strategies you have been introduced to, however, it will help you to recognise the main points of a text as quickly and effectively as possible. It is important to decide why you are reading the text and then to decide on appropriate strategies for finding out what you want from the text.

4 Statistics without tears

The topic of this unit is statistics. Many degree courses involve some knowledge of statistics, either because statistics are often quoted in academic texts, or because students have to work with statistics for their academic assignments. Also, statistics are often used by governments and other organisations to make decisions which can affect all of our lives. From this point of view, some understanding of what it means to think statistically should be useful to everyone.

This unit will give you practice in:

- reading to acquire knowledge;
- distinguishing between main and minor points in a text;
- summarising information from short sections of a text.

Pre-reading task: Statistics in practice

- Discuss the following questions in groups. Do you agree on the answers?

   a) John works in an office. On Monday, he arrived at work at nine o'clock. On Tuesday, he arrived at work at nine o'clock. On Wednesday, he arrived at work at nine o'clock. On Thursday, he arrived at work at nine o'clock. What time do you think he arrived on Friday? Why?

   b) Your friend wants to show you a magic trick. He tosses a coin three times, and each time it falls to the ground with heads facing up. As he goes to toss the coin again, he asks you, *Do you think it will be heads again?* and you say *No*, but when he tosses the coin, it is heads. He tosses the coin twice more, and each time it is heads again. You pick up the coin and look at both sides carefully. What do you expect to see? Why?

- Are you sure you have given the correct answers, or could you be wrong? Is it possible to be absolutely sure about such predictions? Why? Why not?

_____

_____

_____

_____

Text 4–1 | Making sense of experience (Source Book pp. 27–30)

Reading task 1: Identifying main and supporting points

In the discussion tasks you have just completed, you used your everyday knowledge of the world to make judgements about what things are likely or unlikely to be true, in order to make a prediction about the current situation. This is an example of everyday statistical thinking. The text you are going to read looks at what it means to think statistically in order to make predictions. If Statistics sounds like a very difficult topic, don't worry – the text comes from a book called *Statistics without tears*!

1.1   The first section you are going to read is called *Making sense of experience*. Turn to page 27 of the *Reading and Writing Source Book* and read Section 1. Which of the following are main points (main) and which are minor points or examples (minor)? Discuss your answers with the rest of the class.

   a)   We are naturally observant of the things around us.   _____

   b)   Our observations often involve counting or measuring things.   _____

   c)   Our observations may concern how big something is.   _____

   d)   Sometimes our observations concern a single thing.   _____

   e)   Sometimes our observations concern several things.   _____

   f)   Observations may be made about a crop in a field.   _____

   g)   We tend to look for connections among the things we have observed.   _____

1.2   Do not read further than Section 1 in the *Reading and Writing Source Book* for now, but look at the writer's question in lines 29–30. Write down what you think the answer is in one or two sentences. Compare your ideas with the rest of the class.

   _____

   _____

   _____

   _____

   _____

Reading task 2: Continuing to identify main and minor points

2.1   Read the first paragraph of Section 2 of the text (page 28) and see how the writer has answered the question he asked at the end of the previous section. Make sure you understand the writer's answer – it is an important part of what he wants you to learn from the text.

2.2   Finish reading this section. Which of the following are main points (main) and which are minor points or examples (minor)? Discuss your answers with the other members of your group.

   a)   Statistics aims to help us make sense of our observations.   _____

   b)   Statistics aims to help us avoid jumping to conclusions.   _____

   c)   Statistics aims to help us be cautious about making generalisations.   _____

   d)   A field was treated with a certain fertiliser and produced a big crop.   _____

   e)   Perhaps other fields treated with the same fertiliser will produce big crops.   _____

2.3   Look at the writer's question at the end of Section 2 (lines 46–47). Write down what you think the answer is in one or two sentences. Then go on to Reading task 3.

   _____

   _____

   _____

   _____

   _____

Reading task 3: Summarising the key points

3.1 Read the first paragraph of Section 3 of the text (page 29) and see how the writer has answered the question he asked at the end of the previous section. Make sure you understand the writer's answer – it is an important part of what he wants you to learn from the text.

3.2 Finish reading this section. Complete the following summaries of the main ideas by referring to the text. Use a word or phrase from the box below and put the correct number in each gap in the sentences which follow.

1 a certain kind of field	6 likelihood (or 'probability')
2 a mistake	7 more confident
3 correct	8 no 100% certainties
4 different kinds of field	9 experience
5 difficult calculations	10 more scientific

a) It could be _____ to conclude that because one field produced a large crop, other fields treated in the same way will do the same.

b) The more observations we make, the _____ we can be about our generalisations.

c) _____ is a very important concept in statistics.

d) Likelihood (or 'probability') refers to the idea that there are _____ in statistics.

e) _____ treated in a certain way may generally produce a bigger potato-crop, but this may not always happen.

When you have finished, discuss your answers with the other members of your group.

3.3 Look at the writer's question at the end of Section 3 (lines 69–74) of the *Reading and Writing Source Book*. Write down what you think the answer is in one or two sentences. Then go on to Reading task 4.

_____

_____

_____

_____

_____

_____

_____

_____

_____

_____

_____

_____

_____

Reading task 4: Summarising the key points

4.1 Read the first paragraph of Section 4 of the text (page 30) and see how the writer has answered the question he asked at the end of the previous section. Make sure you understand the writer's answer – it is an important part of what he wants you to learn from the text.

4.2 Finish reading this section. Complete the gaps in the following summary of the main points, using words from Section 4:

Statistics involves finding _____ patterns among things we observe. However, we should not assume that _____ will all follow these patterns. The two main concerns of statistics are:

a) summarising our _____ .

b) making _____ based on the resulting summary.

Text 4–2 | **What is statistics?** (Source Book pp. 31–32)

Reading task 1: Concentrating on the main points

Read the next part of *Statistics without tears*, entitled *What is statistics?* Make a list of the main points on a separate sheet of paper. You may find it easier to make three lists, following the divisions shown below. Some examples of main points are already given. When you have finished, compare your list with other members of your group.

> **Lines 1–9**
> Example: *Statistics is used in four different senses.*
>
> **Lines 20–32**
> Example: *Most professional activities use statistical thinking.*
>
> **Lines 33–50**
> Example: *Statistics is used because of uncertainty about our observations.*

You are now going to read another part of the book *Statistics without tears*. This part is called *Descriptive and inferential statistics*, and it is divided into two subsections.

Reading task 1: Note-making practice

1.1 Read the first part of Section 6 of the text *Descriptive and inferential statistics* (page 33). Look at the writer's question at the end of the section. Write down what you think the answer is, in one or two sentences. Compare your ideas with the rest of the class.

_____

_____

_____

_____

_____

_____

_____

_____

_____

_____

_____

1.2 Read the first paragraph of Section 7 of the text (page 34) and see how the writer has answered the question he asked at the end of the previous section. Make sure you understand the writer's answer – it is an important part of what he wants you to learn from the text.

1.3 Read the rest of Section 7. Your reason for reading the section is to find out what the writer says about the distinctions between descriptive and inferential statistics, and the reliability of making generalisations. As you read the text, make notes or annotate parts of the text that you will use to complete a short summary of the main points.

_____

_____

_____

_____

_____

_____

_____

_____

_____

_____

Reading task 2: Recalling information from the text

2.1 Look at the following words:

> **descriptive statistics**   **inferential statistics**   **population generalisation**
>
> **sample**   **observation**   **representative**   **reliability**

Recalling information that you have previously read, is one strategy for improving your understanding of a text. You are going to try out this technique now.

Put away the text and any notes you have made. Find another student to work with. Together, try to recall from memory the main points in this section of the text, using the words above to help you. When you have finished, check through the text again to see if you forgot to recall some important information.

2.2 Write a short summary of the relevant points, using the following two headings:

- Distinctions between descriptive and inferential statistics
- The reliability of making generalisations.

2.3 Discuss and compare your summaries in small groups.

2.4 Compare your summary with the one given to you by your teacher. Have you picked out similar main points?

5 Human activity & climate change

In this unit you will read three texts about climate change and whether Man's activities have had a significant impact on climate change. The texts come from a brochure co-sponsored by the United Nations Environment Programme (UNEP) and the World Meteorological Organisation (WMO).

This unit will give you practice in:

- overviewing a text before starting to read it in order to decide its particular value;
- reading for a specific purpose;
- reading selectively in order to identify those words which might provide information relevant to a specific purpose;
- writing into reading as a way of better understanding a text;
- identifying topic sentences in a text and recognising the supporting sentences;
- text-mapping as a means of helping your understanding of what you have read;
- making use of graphs, figures and tables to help your understanding of a text.

Focus task

Your main reason for reading the three texts which follow is to prepare a set of notes using relevant information from the texts in order to either write an essay or give a presentation about the following topic:

What role has human activity played in causing climate change?

Text 5–1 | Extra-textual information (Source Book p. 36)

Pre-reading task 1: Overviewing the text

The purpose behind *overviewing the text* is to help make quick decisions about the particular value of the text to the reader. Overviewing saves time. Two ways of doing this are given below:

- Briefly look at any other extra-textual information (e.g. the blurb).
- Pay attention to the content of the Introduction.

Can you think of other ways of overviewing the text? List them below.

_____

_____

_____

_____

Pre-reading task 2: What you want to learn from a text

Before starting to read a text, it is worth deciding what you can learn about it. This will save time.

Below is a list of questions which might be asked about a text before reading it. Find the answers by overviewing the whole document.

a) What is the text about?

b) Who is/are the author(s) of the text? What is their background?

c) Why was the text written?

d) What type of text is it?

e) Will the text be useful or relevant for carrying out the Focus task?

Pre-reading task 3: Writing into reading

One effective way of fully understanding a text is to *write your way into reading*. This may help you understand the text better once you read it, because it helps you to activate the knowledge you may already have about the topic. Writing into reading involves writing down your own ideas about the topic before attempting to read about it. This strategy should not occupy too much time, and a good idea is simply to write thoughts down in the form of a list.

3.1 Make a list of human activities that you think might have contributed to climate change.

a) Place a tick (✓) beside any activities that you have had personal experience of.

b) Compare your list with a partner and agree on a master list (i.e. the items on which you both agree).

3.2 Turn to Text 5–2: *Common questions about climate change*.

a) Scan through the contents to find appropriate information about the impact of human activities on climate change.

b) Highlight key information and compare this information with your list (i.e. the items on which you both agree).

Text 5–2 | Common questions about climate change (Source Book pp. 37–38)

You are now going to read the Introduction to this text: *Common questions about climate change*.

Reading task 1: Identifying topic sentences

Identifying topic sentences through position and content can help the reader to quickly grasp the main ideas in a text. Paragraphs often contain a sentence which summarises the main point of each particular paragraph. Sometimes, topic sentences are referred to as *paragraph leaders*. Discuss the following with a partner:

1.1 Where would you expect the topic sentence to appear? The first sentence? The final sentence? In the middle of the paragraph?

1.2 What is the function of the other sentences which appear in each paragraph?

Reading task 2: Understanding the general meaning of a text

2.1 Label all the paragraphs in the Introduction (A–I). Refer to Paragraph A. Pay attention to the sentence beginning *First, however, several issues have to be clarified…* What are the issues? Underline and number these issues (1–3).

2.2 Scan through the text and number the paragraphs 1, 2 or 3, depending on which issue they deal with.

2.3 Which paragraph(s) look(s) ahead to the future?

2.4 What is the purpose of the final paragraph?

Reading task 3: Topic sentences and supporting sentences

In this task, you are required to practise careful reading in order to differentiate the topic sentence from supporting sentences in each paragraph. Careful reading simply means to read most of the words in the text in order to fully understand what is written.

3.1 The purpose of this task is to identify the topic sentences in the Introduction.

3.2 In Paragraph A, the final sentence is underlined – in other words, this is the topic sentence of the paragraph. Why is this the topic sentence of the Introduction? What is the purpose of the first sentence?

3.3 Underline the topic sentences in each of the remaining paragraphs (B–I). With a partner, discuss the role of the other sentences in each paragraph.

Reading task 4: Main points and supporting details

When you are reading, it is useful to differentiate between the main ideas in the text and the supporting ideas or details. According to your understanding of the text, which of the following are (A) main ideas and which are (B) supporting ideas or details?

a) Rapid daily weather changes can occur even in areas of unchanging climate.

b) The Earth's surface temperature would be significantly cooler without a natural greenhouse effect.

c) The effects of the wind and the oceans determine the redistribution of heat over the Earth's surface.

d) Volcanic eruptions have a temporary cooling effect.

e) One of the causes of climate change is human activity.

f) The effects of natural greenhouse gases, combined with human activity, lead to higher average Earth temperatures.

g) The rise in the average global temperature will persist for a long period as a result of Man's activities.

h) The *Second Assessment Report* released by the IPPC is very long and detailed.

Reading task 5: Recalling the text

This task involves *recalling* the contents of the text from memory. The idea behind this reading strategy is that, after reading the text, you write down what you have understood from the text. As a result, you may discover that you have understood more than you originally believed. Secondly, you will more easily recognise gaps in your understanding and recognise which parts of the text to concentrate on when rereading. Your teacher will only give you a few minutes to complete this task, so it is best to write quickly in note form.

5.1 Without looking back at the text, list the main points.

5.2 Compare your list with a partner.

5.3 Agree on a master list (i.e. the items on which you both agree).

_____

_____

_____

_____

_____

_____

_____

5.4 Check with the text. Revise your list if necessary.

5.5 Individually, consider which of the points on your list are relevant to your completion of the Focus task: _What role has human activity played in causing climate change?_ Place a tick (✓) beside all the relevant points you have listed above.

Text 5–3 | Are human activities contributing to climate change? (Source Book pp. 39–41)

You are now going to read the next section of the text: _Are human activities contributing to climate change?_

Reading task 1: Identifying relevant information in a text

1.1 Read through the contents of this section in order to confirm that it will help in the completion of the Focus task: _What role has human activity played in causing climate change?_ As you read, label the paragraphs A–M.

1.2 Re-read Paragraph A. What do you consider is the key point made?

_____

_____

_____

_____

_____

1.3 What word(s) in this first paragraph suggest(s) that this claim should be taken seriously?

_____

1.4 Search through the remaining paragraphs and highlight areas of the text which might be of use in completing the Focus task. NB: Use a pencil to tick (✓) or bracket appropriate sections of the text. Using a highlighter pen initially can be a mistake in case you change your mind about the information at a later stage.

1.5 There is, in fact, a limited amount of information which clearly gives an indication of the contribution of human activity to climate change in this section. Which paragraph(s) clearly state(s) that they do?

1.6 Apart from the concluding sentence in Paragraph M, there is other support for the claim that 'human activity contributes to climate change'. In which paragraphs can you find this?

1.7 In Paragraph B, what suggests the difficulty which scientists have in analysing the problem?

1.8 In Paragraph E, what information might make the reader be concerned about the way the data was collected?

1.9 Referring to Paragraph K, what connection can be made between the comparison of *observed patterns of temperature change* and those *predicted by models* and the role of human activity on global change?

Reading task 2: Detailed reading

There is a significant amount of the text that is not directly relevant to the Focus task – which is the main purpose for reading the document. However, it may be useful to study other parts of the text quite carefully to help your understanding of the topic.

2.1 What is the function of this section of the text, apart from answering the question: *Are human activities contributing to climate change?*

2.2 Complete the following summary by filling the gaps with either one or two words. The words required are all used in the original text.

> # STUDYING CLIMATE CHANGE
>
> Studying the causes of unusual climate change is problematic because change caused by _____ is often hidden or masked by natural climate variability. In order to separate these two factors, investigations can be divided into _____ and _____ studies. In the first case, information can be gained by measuring _____ , and in the second situation by finding reasons for the unusual changes in climate that have been noted. In attributing causes resulting from human activity, scientists can make use of _____ . Two examples of this are, firstly, by comparing maps or patterns of temperature change, which is known as _____ , or secondly, by finding characteristic patterns of climate response between observed climate change and predicted change from models, which is referred to as a _____ .

Reading task 3: Recalling the text from memory

This is a Recall task, which you have practised previously (see page 45).

3.1 Without looking back at the text, list all the key points (based on the main ideas).

Example: **Climate change caused by human activity ➜ e.g. burning fossil fuels.**

Continue your list as quickly as possible, noting down the ideas as you think of them. You can rearrange them later if you wish.

Write your list below.

3.2 Compare your list with another student and agree on a master list. Place a tick (✓) beside the key points you agree on. Refer to the text to consider any further key information that you have omitted.

| Text 5–4 | What human activities contribute to climate change (Source Book pp. 42–43) |

Reading task 1: Making use of figures and tables

Apart from the text, this section contains two figures (Figures 3.1 and 3.2). You can understand a great deal by carefully studying graphs, diagrams, illustrations and tables. Such figures are intended to summarise the contents of what you are reading. By paying attention to these visual aids, you often get a much clearer understanding of the text.

1.1 Study Figure 3.1. With a partner, discuss what conclusions can be made from this diagram. For example, compare the relative importance of climate change caused by carbon dioxide and methane. Also discuss what contributions the greenhouse gases described in Figure 3.1 have made to climate change.

1.2 To what extent does the displayed data help you to answer the question that forms the title of this section – *What human activities contribute to climate change*?

1.3 Read through the text in order to locate the sections that refer specifically to each of the particular gases displayed in Figure 3.1. Underline the names of the gases as you locate them.

Reading task 2: Reading displayed information

Study Figure 3.2. What conclusions can be made about the contents of this figure? Answer the following questions to help you make appropriate conclusions.

2.1 What is the general trend for all three groups of countries?

2.2 Which group of countries was contributing the most to climate change by 1992?

2.3 What future trends are suggested by the graph? Read through the text to find which paragraph(s) are related to Figure 3.2.

Reading task 3: Inferring meaning from a text

3.1 Re-read the text and find references to the following phrases. What is their significance regarding climate change?

Example: **The burning of fossil fuels = very significant contributor to carbon dioxide emissions.**

a) The regrowth of vegetation in the Northern Hemisphere

b) Land use changes

c) Existing international agreements

d) The tropospheric ozone

e) The Antarctic ozone hole

f) Small particles in the atmosphere

3.2 After discussing the significance of the above with a partner and checking the answers with your teacher, decide what general conclusions can be made. Write your conclusion below.

_____

_____

_____

_____

_____

_____

_____

_____

_____

_____

_____

_____

_____

Reading task 4: Making use of a text

You should now be ready to return to the Focus task on the first page of this unit (page 42). Re-read this task and decide what information you can use from the three texts in order to prepare notes for an oral presentation, or a plan for a writing assignment.

What role has human activity played in causing climate change?

4.1 Prepare and organise your notes as directed by your teacher.

4.2 Explain the contents and organisation of your notes to a partner.

4.3 You will now be asked to either give an oral presentation or complete a writing assignment.

The global village

6

In this unit you will read up to six sections of a text called *The global village*. Then you will be asked to carry out a short summarising task. While you are carrying out the tasks related to the text, you will have to decide what information (if any) in each section of the text is relevant to your summary. When you have finished reading all the sections of the text, you will be able to make use of the relevant notes that you have made in order to help you with the summary.

This unit will give you practice in:

- recognising main points in a text;
- reading for a specific purpose;
- analysing the titles, subtitles (subheadings) and other displayed information accompanying the main texts;
- recalling the text to consolidate your understanding;
- comparing your views (as a reader) with those of the writer;
- monitoring your understanding of the text while you are reading.

The term *global village* was first used by the Canadian academic, Marshall McLuhan. What is your understanding of this term? If you haven't heard this term before, what do you think it means?

- Talk to other members of your group. Can you agree on what the term *global village* means? Write down your group's opinion of what it means.

- Compare your group's definition with the definition given to you by your teacher. How similar are they?

- Consider some of the characteristics of the *global village* from the teacher's definition. Make a list of the ways that you think they may have affected your life. For example, you are studying abroad and you may consider this to be a direct (or indirect) result of globalisation. Compare your list with other members of your group.

Text 6–1	Introduction (Source Book pp. 44–45)

Reading task 1: Checking predictions

1.1   Read the Introduction. Find out whether any of the points mentioned by the author are similar to the views you have noted about the effects of globalisation on your life.

1.2   As you read:
- highlight any ideas in the text that are similar to the ones that you have on your list (underline with a <u>solid line</u>).
- highlight any ideas in the text which are not on your list (underline with a <u>broken line</u>).
- compare your answers with a partner.

Text 6–2   The shrinking planet (Source Book pp. 45–46)

Pre-reading task 1: Thinking about the topic

1.1 The title of this section is *The shrinking planet*. What do you think this means?
(Remember that the overall theme of the text is *The global village*.)

_____

_____

_____

_____

_____

_____

_____

_____

_____

_____

1.2 In which ways do trade, tourism and technology lessen the differences between people in different parts of the world?

a) *Global brand names, e.g. Coca–Cola* _____

b) _____

c) _____

d) _____

e) _____

f) _____

1.3 Do you think that some differences between people in different parts of the world may be maintained in spite of globalisation, or even increased because of it? If so, what examples can you think of?

_____

_____

_____

_____

_____

_____

_____

_____

1.4 Look at the words and expressions in the box below, which are from the text you are going to read. Check you understand what they mean, using a dictionary if necessary. Place the words and expressions in the appropriate column in the table below.

~~discontent~~	cultural convergence the Internet grievances
alien modern cultures	universal links superficial
national culture, history and language	common interests
similar products	human peculiarities homogenising effect
customisation of products	local requirements digital technology

For example, **discontent** would probably cause **divergence**.

Convergence	Divergence
	discontent

1.5 Finally, discuss what you think the text will be about with other members of your group.

Reading task 1: Recalling the text from memory

1.1 You are now going to read the text *The shrinking planet*. Look at the subheading, which comes after the title.

    a) What is the function of this subheading and what does it mean?

        _____

        _____

        _____

        _____

        _____

        _____

        _____

        _____

    b) What contrast is suggested by this subheading?

        _____

        _____

        _____

        _____

        _____

        _____

        _____

    c) Read through the text to find out why the writer feels that *many cultural differences persist*.

1.2 Now, in pairs, recall the text from memory by telling each other what you remember. This will help to consolidate your understanding of the text. It will also help you to appreciate what you haven't understood. Some of the words and expressions you looked at before reading the text may help you. They are repeated below:

> discontent   cultural convergence   the Internet   grievances
>
> alien modern cultures   universal links   superficial
>
> national culture, history and language   common interests
>
> similar products   human peculiarities   homogenising effect
>
> customisation of products   local requirements   digital technology

1.3 After finishing the recall activity, check the text to see whether you have omitted anything important, and whether there are any inaccuracies in the information you have noted.

Reading task 2: Checking the text for details

This task will help you to have a more detailed understanding of the text. Read the text again to complete the task below.

If the statement is correct according to the text, write YES. If the statement is not correct, write NO. If you can find no information relating to the statement, write NOT GIVEN.

a) A surprising number of people in the world are able to watch TV.

b) In 1998, Ronaldo, a young Brazilian footballer, was much better known internationally than President Clinton.

c) Increasing numbers of Africans are migrating to the United States.

d) Some people use the Internet as a method for making political protests.

e) Books about Canada are frequently written in Spanish.

f) There is a football team in Tanzania which has adopted the name Manchester United.

g) An increasing number of young people in China have little or no knowledge of their national heritage.

h) As a result of computer technology, more and more people throughout the world are driving exactly the same basic model of car.

i) Digital technology seems to be reversing the effect of globalisation.

j) The writer is negative about the effects of globalisation.

Reading task 3: Making use of the text content

3.1 Assuming that you are part of *the global village*, what cultural differences persist in your class (if any)?

- Discuss this in groups, and note the results of your discussion in the table below.
- The data you gather may be useful in carrying out the summarising activity which is introduced in the next task (on page 56).

Attitude about:	The same attitude?	Different attitude?
Study methods		
Studying abroad		
Entertainment		
Foreign goods		
International languages		
National culture		

3.2 What conclusions can be drawn from the data you have collected?

_____

_____

_____

_____

Reading task 4: Reading for a purpose

The aim of this Focus task is to provide an overall purpose for using **all** the texts in this unit. It will provide practice in making decisions about what to read and how carefully to read it. It will also provide an opportunity to practise your note-taking techniques.

Your task is to complete the following activity based on your reading of the texts.

Has social diversity generally increased as the result of economic globalisation?

Based on your own experience and the experience of other members of your group, to what extent do you agree that social diversity has generally increased? What evidence exists in the texts to support your answer?

4.1 Think about the most appropriate way to carry out this task, and then discuss your ideas in small groups.

4.2 Look through all the sections of this unit (including any sections not yet referred to) and decide which parts of each section you could use to complete the assignment, i.e. you are looking for relevant information.

4.3 Underline ideas in each section which appear to support the statement with a single solid line, and ideas that do not support the statement with a broken line.

4.4 What ideas have the title of the assignment and your reading of all the texts given you about what should be included in the summary? Individually or with other members of your group, make a list (in an appropriate note form). Remember to consider the data you collected in Task 3 on page 55.

_____

_____

_____

_____

Text 6–3 | Economic globalisation (Source Book pp. 46–49)

The aim of this section is to look more closely at the text and decide how relevant the content is with regard to completing the Focus task outlined above. This is also an opportunity to reconsider the highlighting/note-taking you carried out above – you may wish to change or add to your highlighting as you go through this section. The text is divided into the main body (paragraphs A–H) and three sets of accompanying notes: _The global marketplace_; _Competition and protection_; and _Global financial markets_.

Reading task 1: Asking questions about the text

One way of getting a better understanding of the text when reading carefully is to ask yourself questions about the text as you read.

1.1 Look at the following questions. As you read the text, underline the words or phrases which answer these questions. When you have finished, check your answers with the teacher.

a) What inconsistency is expressed in the section entitled *The global marketplace*? (Use no more than 10 words.)

b) What two things have increased dramatically because of economic globalisation? (2 things)

c) What services, mentioned in paragraph B, have been *globalised*? (2 services)

d) What international agreements and organisations have affected economic globalisation? (3)

e) What has hampered economic globalisation? (4 factors)

f) What is done in some countries to protect the workforce?

g) Why does the expansion of international trade cause even some well-managed businesses to fail?

h) In what ways is the pre-industrial village different from the global village? (Use no more than 10 words.)

i) Which countries benefit most from economic globalisation?

j) What positive long-term factors does the writer identify in the final paragraph?

k) In what ways has economic globalisation had a negative effect on richer countries? (3 points – use no more than 10 words per point.)

1.2 Can you think of any other questions you could ask that would help your understanding of the text?

1.3 Finally decide, with a partner, how relevant your answers are to the Focus task.

Reading task 2: Identifying key information in the text

This task will help you to check your understanding of the main point of each paragraph in the text *Economic globalisation*.

The main body of the text is divided into eight paragraphs, which have been labelled A–H. Below there is a list of sentences that summarise each of the above paragraphs. Your task is to match each of the summarising sentences (1–8) with the appropriate letter.
Example: **Paragraph A = Sentence 3**.

A = 3	B = ___	C = ___	D = ___	E = ___	F = ___	G = ___	H = ___

Summary sentences

1)   There are a number of factors which may delay the process of globalisation.

2)   The differences between people become less important as a result of economic globalisation.

3)   Several corporate household names exemplify current global trends.

4)   International free trade is directed by global agreements and covers a far greater range of commodities than was traditional.

5)   The developed world continues to dominate the process of globalisation.

6)   Economic power does not necessarily dictate policy when human issues stand in its way.

7)   The size of foreign investment and the globalisation of service industries are clearly demonstrated in most areas of the world.

8)   Concentration of economic power is tending to cause greater tension between the rich and the poor.

Reading task 3: Preparing to complete the Focus task

3.1   Review the answers to Reading tasks 1 and 2.

3.2   Revise your list of points relevant to the Focus task (see page 56: 4.4) so that any new points you have found are incorporated in your list.

3.3   Compare your lists with each other by referring to the text where necessary.

Text 6–4 Community & conflict (Source Book pp. 49–51)

The next text consists of a main body (Paragraphs A–H) and three short accompanying texts which provide further comment on the topic. These are in separate boxes.

The purpose of reading this section was initially to decide whether it is relevant to the assignment outlined on page 56 (Task 4), i.e. 'Social diversity has generally increased as the result of economic globalisation.'

Pre-reading task: Thinking about the topic

The text outlines some of the social effects that globalisation has had on individual societies. You may wish to make notes about this and/or discuss the title with other members of your group.

- Think about the title *Community & conflict*. What does this suggest about the contents of the section?

- Compile a list of five causes of conflict in modern society on an international/global scale, so that later you can compare this list with references to conflict made in the text. For example, one cause of dispute on an international scale may be the borders between two countries where one or both countries accuse the other of *stealing* some of their land.

- With reference to the title, what *community* do you suppose the writer is referring to? Read the subtitle and the note *Global village – global inequality*. What implication is made regarding the possibility of conflict?

Reading task 1: Developing understanding of the text

1.1 The subtitle refers to the citizens of the global village. Who are the citizens of the global village? While reading the text, highlight any words or phrases which might indicate certain characteristics/features of the typical *citizen*. (Example: *better educated*)

1.2 Make brief notes of the types of global community mentioned.

Reading task 2: Identifying relevant information in the text

2.1 Read through the text and highlight/annotate sections of the text which relate to conflict.

2.2 Compare your annotations with the list you compiled for the pre-reading task for this section. Decide whether the points on your list are similar to the points raised in the text.

2.3 Now discuss this with other members of your group.

Reading task 3: Identifying information relevant to the Focus task

You now have to decide whether the contents of this section are relevant to the Focus task assignment (page 56). Do you think that the social diversity mentioned in this section of the text is a result of the globalisation of business and trade?

Think about the causes of conflict mentioned in the text, using the areas of the text you have already highlighted.

3.1 In what ways, if any, are the points you have highlighted related to the globalisation of business and trade?

3.2 List any points which you consider relevant in order to share with another group.

_____

_____

_____

_____

_____

_____

_____

Reading task 4: Deciding on the relevance of further related texts

Write a two-paragraph summary of the main ideas you would use to complete the following assignment for a university lecturer:

Has social diversity generally increased as a result of economic globalisation?

To what extent do you think social diversity has increased? What evidence exists with reference to the texts selected from *The global village: Challenges for a shrinking planet*.

4.1 You might try *recalling* the texts immediately after reading them to check your understanding.

4.2 You might also decide to ask yourself questions as you are reading through the texts (as you practised with Text 6–3, Task 1, page 57).

4.3 It may also be useful to identify topic sentence(s) or main idea(s) in each paragraph, etc.

4.4 You might decide to *skim* through the texts first and then read them more carefully (or selected parts which seem more relevant) and annotate certain key ideas or words.

Text 6–5	The sharing of sovereignty (Source Book pp. 51–53)

Text 6–6	Converging or diverging? (Source Book pp. 53–55)

Two more texts from the same source follow: *The sharing of sovereignty* (Text 6–5) and *Converging or diverging?* (Text 6–6). You must decide for yourself how useful these texts are and whether to use them or not. You may find it useful to employ some of the reading strategies that you have already practised with the first four texts in this unit and in earlier units. For example, consider the reading strategies in 4.1–4.4 above.

7 The new linguistic order

In this unit you are going to read an article written by Joshua A. Fishman called *The new linguistic order*, which appeared in the journal *Foreign Policy* (1998). You will make use of the contents of the Fishman article to complete an assignment. Thus, you will be approaching a text in the same way in which you will be expected to deal with reading on many academic courses. You are, in fact, 'reading to learn' rather than 'learning to read'.

This unit will give you practice in:

- making use of a specific text to support your ideas;
- some of the skills you have been using on this Reading course.

Assignment

What future significant language developments might occur in a country such as Zambia?

Discuss this topic with special reference to the text *The new linguistic order*.

Pre-reading task: Deciding how to read a text

You will have to make certain decisions about how to approach the article. For example, you need to be selective about the information which you will make use of. Obviously, the information should be relevant to the assignment you have to complete. This should lead you to making decisions about how to read the article.

- Should you, for example, read straight through the article first before making any notes, or should you annotate the text as you read?

- Should you look quickly at the headings in the text and read only the parts which seem relevant to the title of the assignment?

- Should you check every word you don't understand? If not, how should you deal with unknown vocabulary?

- What other decisions do you need to make? Individually or in small groups, take a few minutes to decide about this.

Reading task 1: Reading an introductory case study

1.1 Before reading the main article, you are going to read a short text and discuss the importance of English in Zambia and what future English will have in countries like Zambia. This short text provides some background information relevant to the current use of English in Zambia. Read through the introduction about Zambia below and make note of four points about the language situation in Zambia which you consider to be particularly important or interesting.

LANGUAGES IN ZAMBIA

Zambia is a developing landlocked country situated in Central Africa. The population, approximately 9.7 million, is made up of 98.7% African people, 1.1% European and 0.2% other (*The World Factbook*, 1999 – Zambia). The African population consists of four main tribal groups. There are also a number of subsidiary groups. As a result, there is a wide variety of tribal languages and dialects. There is also a significant number of other permanent residents in Zambia whose first-language is not a Zambian tribal language or dialect. For example, there are first-language speakers of English, Swahili, Hindi and Afrikaans. Because of this, it has been necessary for Zambia to have a common language of communication for a range of social, political, educational, technical and economic reasons. Zambia is part of Anglophone Africa, and therefore the common language (lingua franca) is English. Approximately 78% of the population over the age of 15 can read and write English. There are also at least seven major vernacular languages that dominate and approximately 70 other indigenous languages.

Zambia is surrounded by neighbouring countries, each having a major European lingua franca as well as official tribal languages. These countries are Tanzania, Malawi, Zimbabwe and Namibia, where the lingua franca is English; Angola and Mozambique (Portuguese) and the Democratic Republic of Congo (formerly Zaire), where the lingua franca is French. In all these countries, like Zambia, therefore, there is multilingualism, e.g. Zambians communicate through the lingua franca as well as through at least one of the official vernacular languages. Several of the local languages transcend borders. For example, Bemba is spoken in Northern Zambia and in the south of the Democratic Republic of Congo; Nyanja in Eastern Zambia and Malawi, etc.

1.2 In groups of two to four students, compare the points you have picked out as important or interesting. As a class, check which points have been most frequently selected. Now discuss the possible significance of the following:

- The existence of other lingua francas on Zambia's borders.

- Local languages that overlap the borders of Zambia and her neighbours.

- Local languages that continue to be spoken by the vast majority of Zambians.

1.3 Look at the following possible developments and prioritise them in order from *most likely* to *least likely*. Discuss the order you have chosen with other students.

IN THE FUTURE

A English will take over entirely as the only language spoken in Zambia.

B Language conflicts will develop between English speakers and other language communities.

C English will become increasingly the language of the elite, and non-fluent speakers will be seriously disadvantaged.

D The situation is likely to remain as it is, i.e. multilingualism with languages co-existing in order to serve different purposes.

E English will be replaced by some other official language.

1.4 Now, you are going to read the article *The new linguistic order*. As you are reading, keep thinking about what information would be relevant for completing the following assignment:

What future significant language developments might occur in a country such as Zambia?

Discuss this topic with special reference to the text *The new linguistic order*. You will need to make notes as you are reading. You need to make decisions about how to do this. By the end of this unit, you will be expected to have produced notes on part of the text relevant to the assignment. However, at this stage you will study the first part of the text in shorter stages.

Text 7–1 | The new linguistic order (Source Book pp. 56–64)

Reading task 1: Understanding subject-specific vocabulary

1.1 Turn to the text *The new linguistic order*. In the first three paragraphs of the text, the following words or phrases appear:

1) mother tongue	2) globalization	3) official language
4) regionalization	5) local language	

Read through the first three paragraphs, find these words or phrases and match them with the definitions given on page 65.

a) A process in which a language is used in neighbouring countries, particularly for business or official reasons, but also for educational, social or recreational purposes.

b) This is used for business, in government and law courts; it may also be the national language.

c) Used in part of a country or region mostly as a first language, usually for personal, social or commercial reasons; sometimes for official or educational reasons.

d) The first language to be acquired at home.

e) A process involving worldwide interaction in trade, politics, recreation, education, etc.

1.2 It is normal in an academic situation for a student to have a *working* vocabulary of a particular subject or topic which has been picked up either from the lecture or seminar environment or from a handout or some other source of information. Such a working vocabulary of subject-specific words should help the reader's understanding of any relevant text they are asked to read. The following terms (1–10) all appear in the text. Which of them do you already understand? In groups, discuss what these terms mean.

Match the terms in the box below with the definitions (a–j) that follow.

> **1) first language**   **2) pidgin**   **3) multilingual**   **4) lingua franca**
>
> **5) vernacular**   **6) minority language**   **7) working language**
>
> **8) immersion language**   **9) neologism**   **10) standardised language**

Match the following definitions with the terms (1–10) above:

a) An internationally used language of communication, e.g. English or French in Africa.

b) Referring to a language spoken by a significant number of the population (for example, a tribal language), but not the official or national language.

c) The use of three or more languages by an individual or a group of speakers.

d) A language used 'comfortably' by speakers for specific purposes, e.g. for study, trade or diplomacy.

e) A language which is systematically introduced throughout a country or region, usually by the government.

f) A language which is convenient when speakers of different languages need to communicate; usually with a limited vocabulary and grammatical structure.

g) A variety of the language which has the highest status in a nation, usually based on the speech and writing of educated native speakers of the language.

[ ]

h) This usually refers to the language that a user feels most comfortable with. It is normally acquired at home or through the influence of, for example, school.

[ ]

i) A newly invented word or phrase in a particular language.

[ ]

j) A language spoken by relatively few people, for example, in one country or because the number of speakers anywhere is relatively small.

[ ]

You can check the answers in a dictionary and then with your teacher. Later, when reading the text, you can refer back to the definitions above for clarification.

Reading task 2: Predicting content to help understanding

2.1 Reread the introduction to the text (Paragraphs A–C, *Reading and Writing Source Book* page 57).

- From reading the first three paragraphs, what do you think the rest of the article will be about? You will notice that this particular article does not have a list of contents, but your teacher will show you how to devise a contents list of your own. This will serve as an outline and help you to approach your reading more efficiently.

The article will be about:

_____

_____

_____

_____

_____

_____

_____

_____

_____

_____

_____

_____

_____

_____

_____

_____

_____

_____

2.2   Think of certain questions which you would like the article to answer in relation to the assignment. By doing this, you will be able to focus more easily on the parts of the article which are most relevant to the assignment.

Example: **Why has English become such an influential language in a country like Zambia?**

In the box below, write down a list of similar questions based on your reading of paragraphs A–C and on the background information on Zambia (page 63 of this Course Book).

Check your questions with other students and with the teacher.

Questions about the text:

Why has English become a global language?

Reading task 3: Selecting relevant information from the text

By now, you should be ready to carry out the main reading task. You have made decisions about how to read the article and what information you hope to learn from it.

- Begin reading the article in the way you have decided is the most appropriate.

- Collect relevant information by making notes in the way you think will be most useful.

- Your teacher will give you a time limit for reading and for collecting the relevant information. At the end of the time limit, you will have read at least some of the text. After reading and collecting information within the specified time limit, form groups with other students and compare the notes you have made so far.

- Check the information you have agreed on with the teacher.

- Continue reading and making notes in whichever form you decide is most appropriate, until you have finished the article.

- Repeat as above, if necessary, i.e. collecting information and collating with other students and then checking with the teacher.

Reading task 4: Fulfilling your reading purpose

● Use the notes you have made to write an extended paragraph in answer to the following question:

What future significant language developments might occur in a country such as Zambia?

● Discuss this topic with special reference to the text *The new linguistic order*.

● One way of tackling this writing assignment is to turn back to the prioritising task (1.3) you carried out on page 64 of this Course Book.

● Would you still prioritise the developments in the same way that you did at that stage? Why or why not?

● Use the information in the text to decide what your answer to the question is, and write your assignment accordingly.